# Goat the Goat

Margaret Mahy
Illustrated by Trish Hill

## CELEBRATION PRESS
Pearson Learning Group

"Mom, we're bored!" complained Annie.

"It seems as though the summer vacation has been going on forever!" exclaimed Mom, as she packed the dishwasher—again. "The mess! And kids everywhere!"

"There's only two of us *now*," said Alan.

"For the moment," said Mom.

"Why don't you go and play in the park?" suggested Dad. "You could take some photos with your new camera."

Alan patted the camera hanging around his neck as he looked through the window and across the road at the stretch of green that was the park. Off to one side he could see the swings and the great long slide and the playground maze.

Oddly enough, at that time of day the park seemed to be empty. Still, no doubt Bad Brian Beaker was there, somewhere, lurking about. He always was.

"But Bad Brian Beaker hangs out in the playground,"
said Annie before Alan could. "He jumps out of the
maze and threatens Alan. We've *told* you and *told* you."

"Just threaten him back!" said Dad, straightening his shoulders and trying to look threatening himself. "You just have to look scary!"

Alan sighed.

"But Brian Beaker is really big," said Annie. "He's huge. He's even got hairy arms and legs."

"You kids are very hard on Brian," said Mom. "I've talked to him. He's a bit rough—I'll give you that—but he's not so bad really. He speaks very nicely."

"To grown-ups and teachers maybe," said Alan.

"He knows a nice voice will trick you," said Annie.

Alan could tell Mom was going to argue. Adults did not believe kids could trick them. But at this moment Dad let out a shout.

"Look!" he cried. "There by the gate! It can't be!"

Annie and Alan and Mom all looked through the window. They could not see the park any more. A battered blue bus with daisies painted along its side had pulled up in front of their house. The painted daisies spelled out the words "Happy Days".

"This just has to be one of the Uncles," cried Dad.

"One of the odd Uncles," said Alan.

"The Great ones," said Annie.

Dad had seven uncles, and they were all Great Uncles of Alan and Annie.

But as they stared, a little old woman came walking around the back of the blue bus and onto the sidewalk. She stared at the number on the mailbox, then smiled a smile that somehow skipped up the garden path and slipped in under the front door.

"Great Aunt Sylvia!" said Dad. "She's a real gypsy. Haven't heard from her for ages."

"I wonder what sort of dog she's got in that bus," said Annie a little nervously.

"Oh come on! She may not even have a dog," said Dad.

"I'll bet she has," said Alan. "They all have dogs . . . every one of them. Great Uncle Clark had a snappy, yappy little dog . . ."

"And Great Uncle Cuthbert had a dog as big as a bear," said Annie. "And Great Uncle Paul had a dog that caught frisbees . . ."

". . . and then ran away with them," said Alan, remembering.

"She's opening the back of the bus," said Annie. "What's coming out?"

Something was trotting out of the bus and into the sunshine.

"A white dog," said Dad, but sounding as if he was not too sure of himself.

"A tall white dog with a red collar," said Mom. "Oh dear!"

"A dog with a beard," cried Alan as if he could not believe what he was seeing.

"Aunt Sylvia's dog is a goat!" shouted Annie.

Great Aunt Sylvia walked briskly up the path, and her goat followed her. It tried to snatch sideways at Mom's lavender, but Great Aunt Sylvia caught it by its red collar. They danced up the path side-by-side.

Dad flung open the front door and held out his arms.

"Sylvia," he cried, "What a surprise!"

Great Aunt Sylvia gave him a hug. Then she hugged Mom. Then she gave Great-Aunt hugs to Alan and Annie. She was certainly good at hugging.

The goat did not hug anyone—it simply watched them out of yellow eyes. It followed them into the sitting room, snatching a leaf from the potted plant as it trotted past. Then it tried to taste a tassel dangling from one of the best pillows, but Great Aunt Sylvia snatched up the pillow and held it over her head.

"Forgive her," said Great Aunt Sylvia, holding the pillow high. "She just wants to wander around and taste things. She's so sick of being cooped up in the back of the bus."

"What's her name?" asked Annie looking at the goat rather uncertainly.

"Goat!" said Great Aunt Sylvia. "It's easy to remember. Goat the goat! Have you got a clothes line at the back of the house? You could tie her to the clothes line. I mean Goat is a well-behaved goat, but she does tend to get into trouble, even indoors."

Great Aunt Sylvia continued, "Goat thinks your curtains look tasty, I can tell. Take her into the backyard, and tie her to the clothes line." Great Aunt Sylvia paused. "But watch out—Goat sometimes eats the wash."

"Better still, take her across the road to the park," said Dad. "Plenty of goat room there and there are no clothes."

"You're not allowed to take pets into the park!" cried Alan. "There are signs that tell you not to."

"Those signs say 'No dogs allowed' and 'No horses allowed' and 'No motorbikes allowed'," said Dad. "They don't mention goats."

Annie began tugging on Goat's red collar.

"This way!" she called. Goat did not move. She did not want to leave Great Aunt Sylvia. She planted her hooves in the living room carpet and stayed where she was.

"Come on, Goat!" shouted Annie impatiently.

   And suddenly Goat shifted. She tightened up. She put her head down and turned her curving brown horns towards Annie.

   "No, no, no," said Great Aunt Sylvia, speaking in a very gentle voice. "Always talk to Goat in a calm, quiet way. If she hears someone sounding angry, she sometimes turns fierce. We don't want that."

   "No way," said Mom quickly.

   "Would she hurt us with her horns?" asked Alan.

   Great Aunt Sylvia stroked Goat's horns.

   "Oh no," she said. "See how her horns curve back? She just curves over any enemies. But she is very strong. Nobody wants to have a powerful goat curving over them. So speak in happy voices. She likes happiness."

Great Aunt Sylvia slapped Goat's bony hip.

"Get along, Goat!" she said in a jolly voice, and this time Goat followed Alan and Annie out of the living room door, then through the front door into the front yard.

"Only a crazy Great Aunt would bring a goat into the house," grumbled Alan.

"I wish *I* had a goat," said Annie. "I wish we had two . . . one each."

The park across the road was sunny, but the trees and bushes around its edges were stirring with wind. Luckily there were no curtains or pillows with tassels. Leaves rustled. Shadows danced across one another. All seemed peaceful.

Suddenly a figure leapt out of the maze. They knew at once who it must be. Brian Beaker, the biggest bully in the street, came swig-swaggering toward them.

"Hey! Look!" he shouted. "A gang of goats." He must have thought it was funny because he shouted it again and again. "A gang of goats! A gang of goats!"

Alan paused. He felt like a real fool, facing Brian Beaker with a goat trotting behind him.

"Leave us alone," yelled Annie. "We're taking our goat for a walk around the park."

Brian Beaker shouted even more. He had had a lot of practice at shouting.

"Beeeeehhh!!" he bleated.

"You sound more like a goat than Goat does," Annie shouted. Alan wished she'd stop that. Brian Beaker sometimes teased her, but he was never nasty or threatened her the way he often did with Alan.

"I'll goat you!" yelled Brian. "I'll really goat you this time!"

Somewhere beside Alan, Goat began to shuffle its hooves. "I'll goat all you goats!" Brian Beaker yelled. "This is MY playground!"

His smile became a scowl. He bounded towards them, trying to catch them. Goat began to dance a little.

"Bambi Beaker," shouted Annie. "Bambi Beaker!"

"Be quiet, Annie," hissed Alan. He knew what a bully Brian Beaker could be.

"Don't call me Bambi!" howled Brian Beaker. He was almost on them. "Call me Basher!" he yelled furiously. "Call me Basher-the-Camera-Smasher."

Something shot past Annie and Alan, charging toward
Brian Beaker. Then Brian Beaker was knocked over
backward into a big bed of begonias. He flopped over
and his feet flew up in the air. All of a sudden Goat was
eying him fiercely.

Brian shouted out in fear, and Alan grabbed Goat's red collar. Goat backed off, but Brian cried, "Get that goat away from me!" Before he could stand up, Goat began licking his face.

"She won't hurt you," Alan assured him.

"Stop crying," Annie said calmly. "Then she'll stop." She grabbed Goat's red collar on one side. Alan grabbed it on the other.

"Make her stop now!" yelled Brian Beaker.

And suddenly Alan had an inspiration. He let go of Goat's collar, stepped back, lifted his camera and (quick as a wink) snapped a photograph of Brian Beaker trembling among the begonias.

click!

"Say 'Please'," said Annie. "Goat likes people to be polite to her."

Brian Beaker looked into Goat's yellow eyes.

"OK. Please!" he begged. "Please! Please!"

Alan and Annie pulled Goat backward between them. Brian Beaker cowered in the flower bed.

"Get out while you can," said Annie. "We might not be able to hold her back for much longer."

Brian Beaker bounded up from among the begonias
and raced away across the park.

Again, as quick as a wink, Alan photographed Brian Beaker running away from him.

"He'd better not try threatening me again," he said. He patted his camera. "He won't want anyone to see my photographs."

Then Alan and Annie took Goat for a run around the park. She trotted along between them, and they let her nibble grass every now and then but stopped her when she made for the flower beds. Then they went back across the park, past the blue bus and turned in at their gate with Goat following them like a good goat.

It was lunchtime, and it turned out that Great Aunt Sylvia had brought some delicious pies as well as a white goat. One way and another it had turned out to be a really exciting summer morning.